The Number Eleven

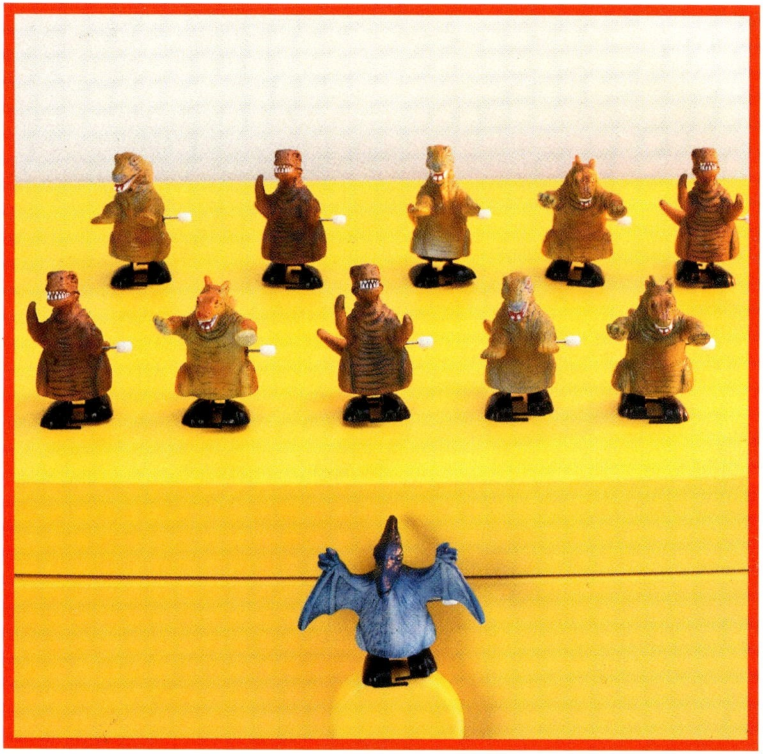

Barbara Taragan

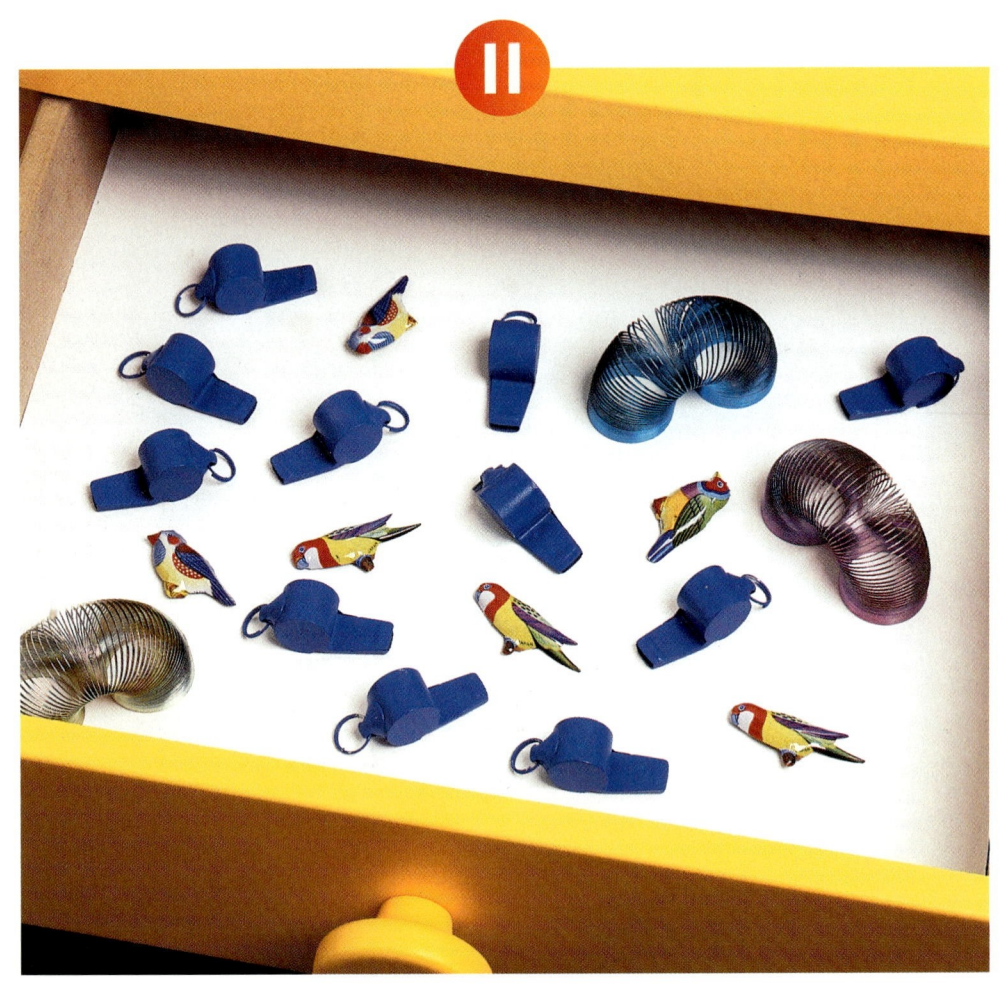

Find eleven blue whistles.

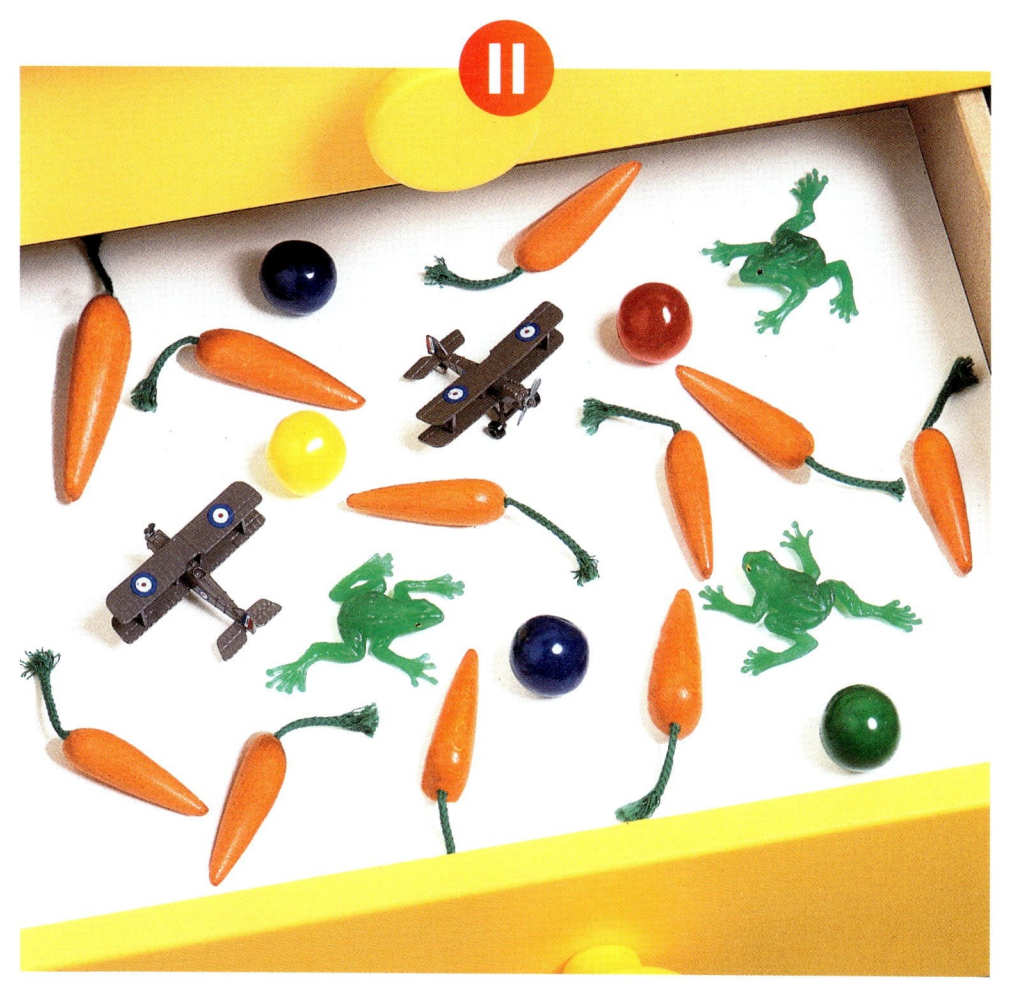

Find eleven orange carrots.

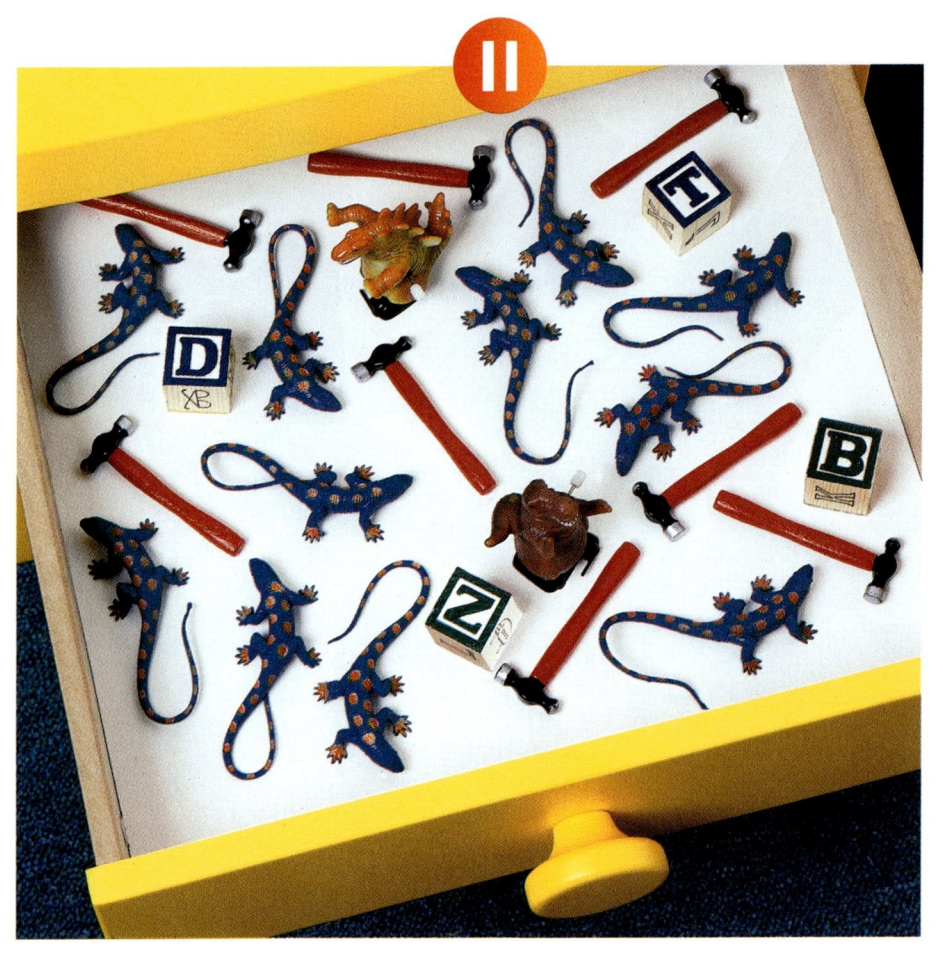

Find eleven purple lizards.

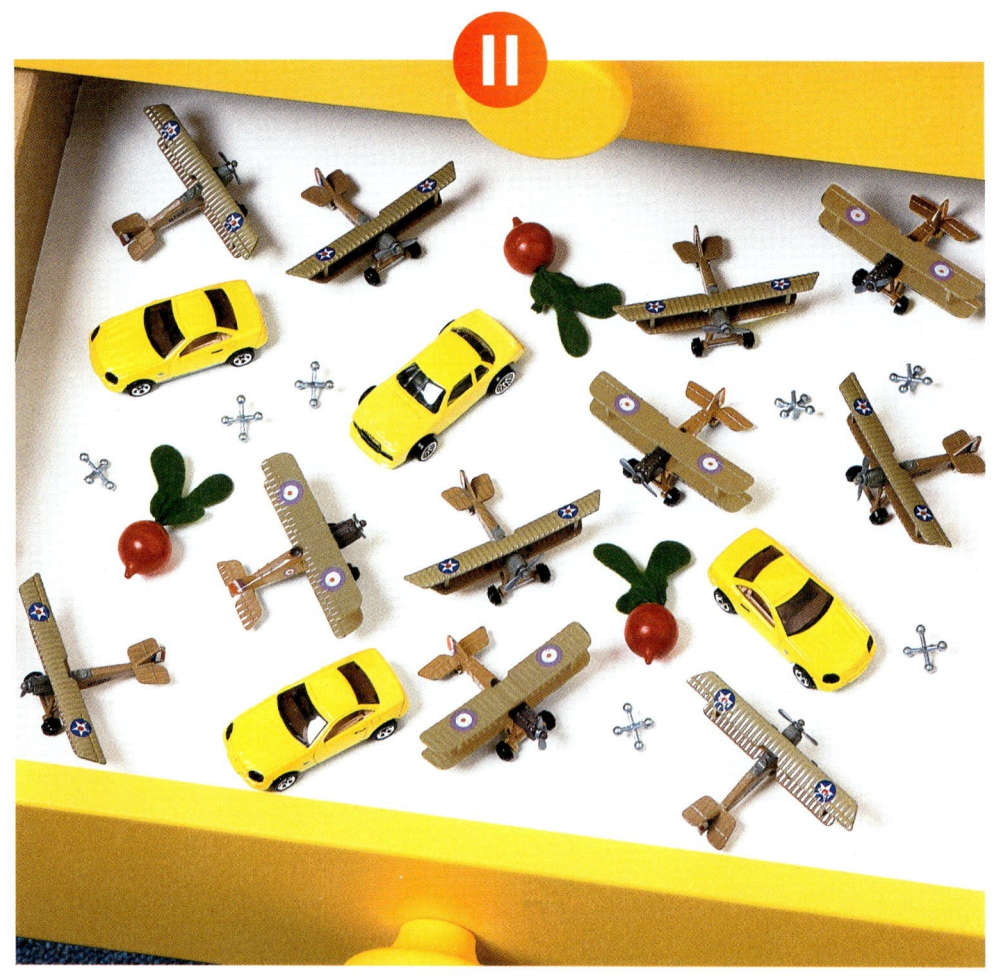

Find eleven brown airplanes.

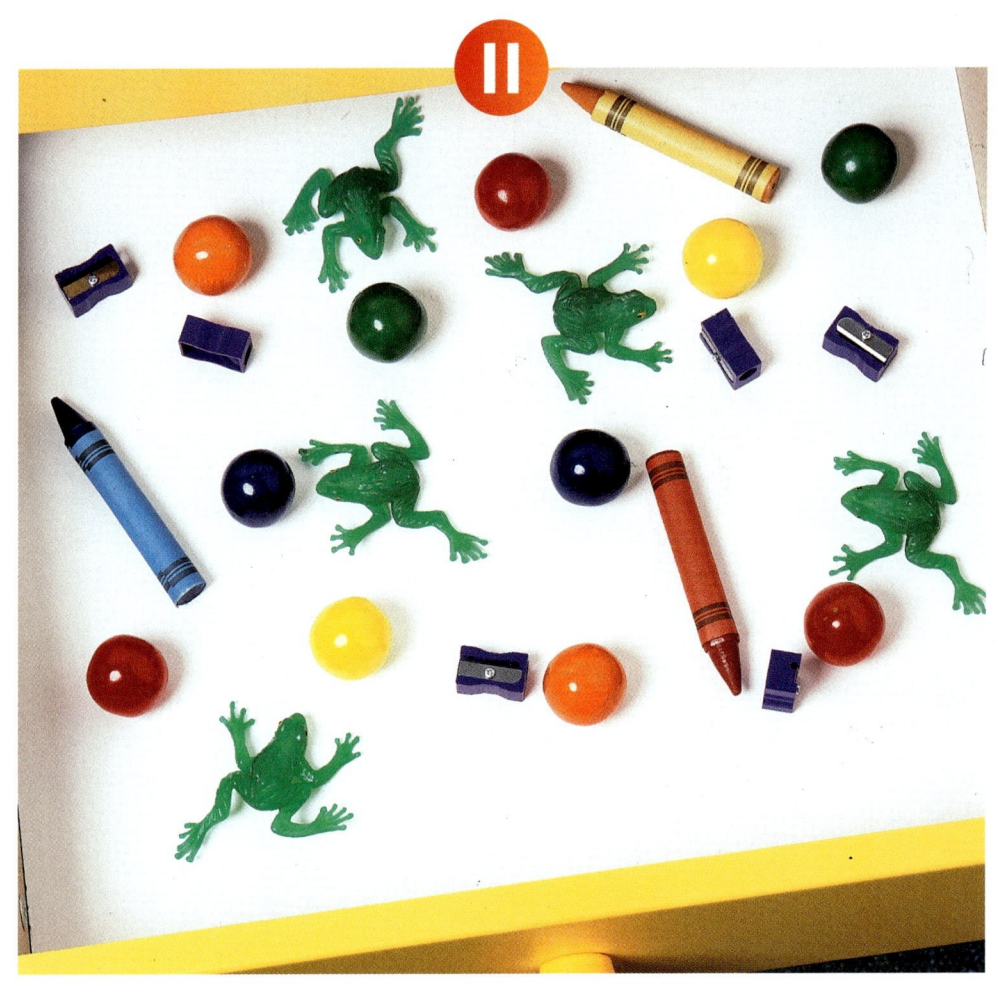

Find eleven balls.

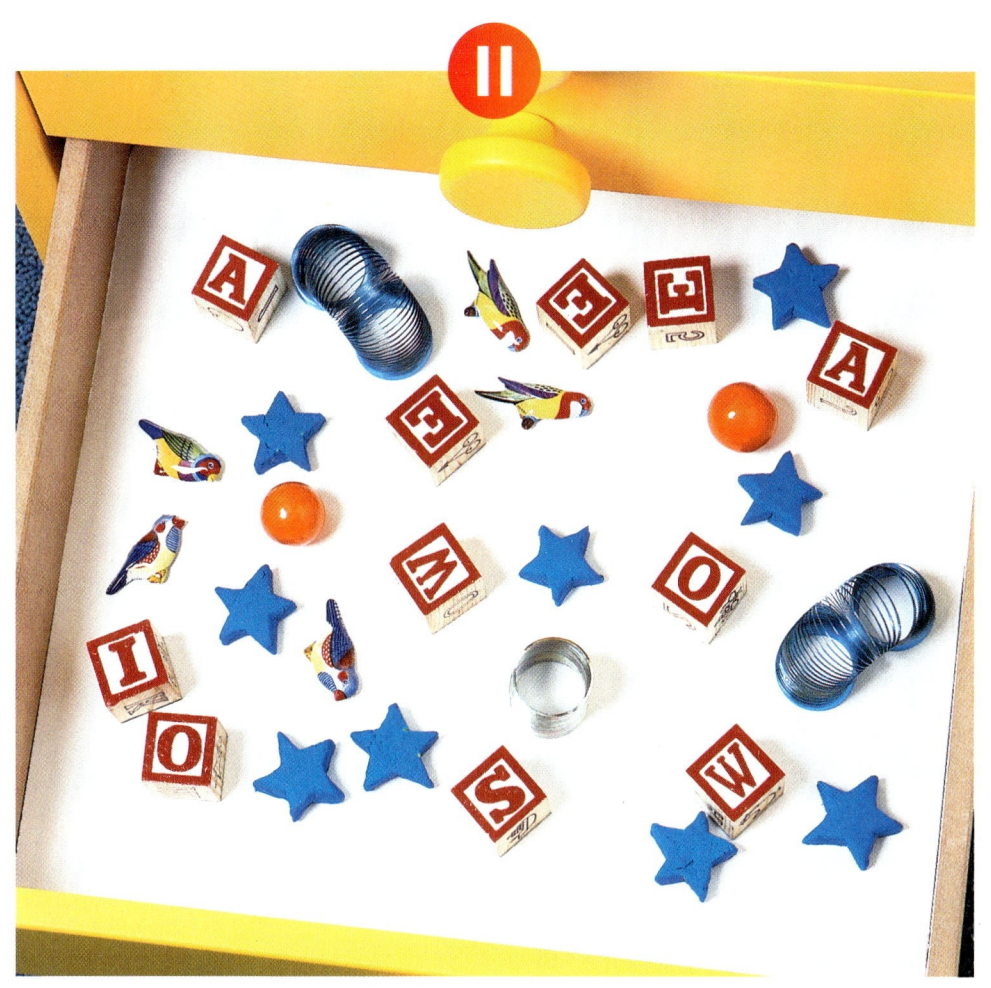

Find eleven blocks.

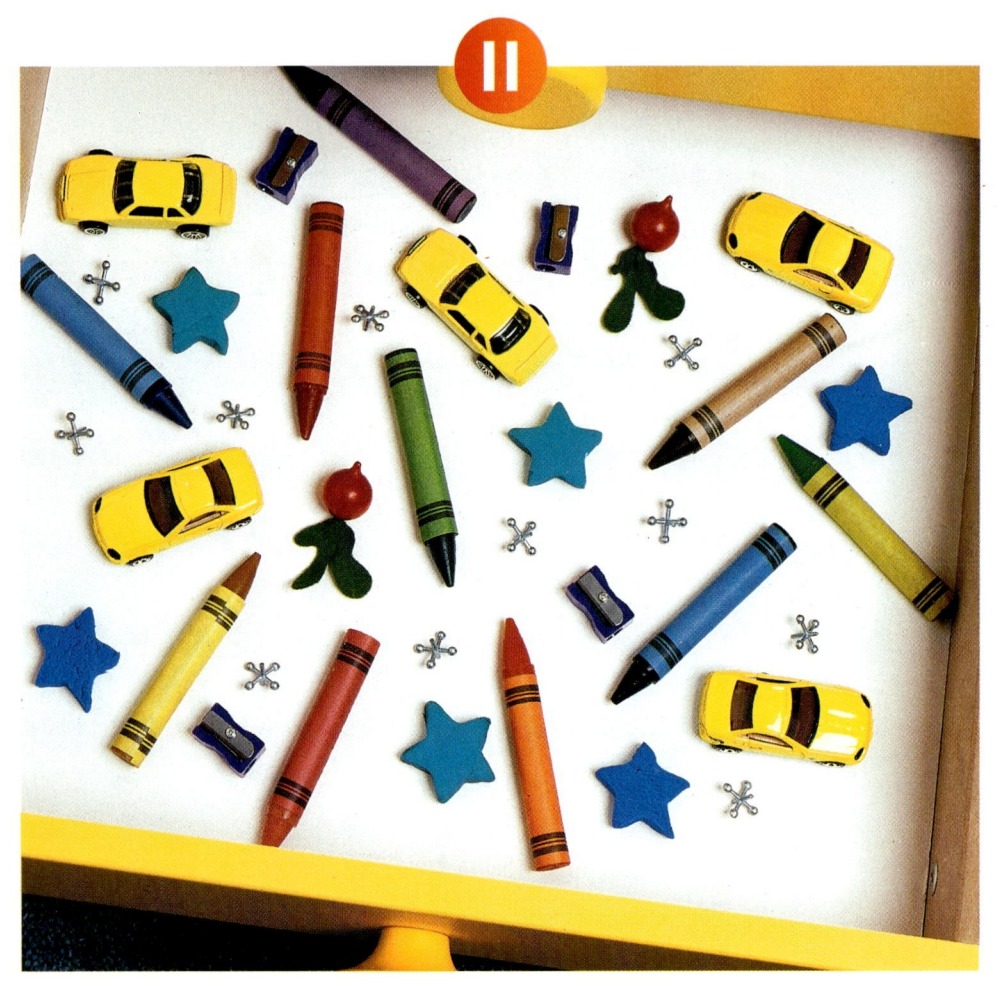

Find eleven of one thing.